My Story
God's Glory

Samantha Williams

My Story, God's Glory
Copyright © 2021 by Samantha Williams
ISBN Print Book: 979-8753821539
All rights reserved.

No part of this book may be used or reproduced by any means, graphic, electronic, or mechanical, including photocopying, recording, taping, or by information storage retrieval system without the publisher's written permission except in the case of brief quotation embodied in critical articles and reviews.

Unless otherwise indicated, all scripture, quotations are taken from the King James Version of the Bible.

Cover Created By: Shekinah Glory Publishing

Shekinah Glory

shekinahglorypublishing.com
(936) 314-7458

Dedication

I dedicate this book to my best friend and Savior, Jesus Christ. When I had nobody, you heard my cry! Thank you!

To my mom, Pamela Williams, your love for God, no matter what happened in your life, and your will to push through did not go unnoticed. You taught me everything I know. I love you and thank you for being you.

To My children, Darien, Lil OJ, Carlos DeAndre, O'terius, and Jaala, I love you all to the moon and back. Being your mother has been nothing short of a blessing.

Finally, to Chris Johnson, your love for me has gone beyond words. Your support and excitement to see me win are unmatched. I thank God for sending you into my life.

I would also like to dedicate this book to every woman who thinks she can't. You can, the end!

Table of Contents

Samantha's Heart
9

Chapter One
It's Story Time
13

Chapter Two
A Weak Foundation
21

Chapter Three
Saved By Grace
35

Chapter Four
Underdeveloped
47

Chapter Five
Trusting In The Lord
59

Chapter Six
Beware Of The Cult
67

Chapter Seven
Another Hurdle To Cross
77

Chapter Eight
Still Searching
83

Chapter Nine
Changing The Narrative
93

Author Bio
107

Samantha's Heart
A LETTER TO HIS PEOPLE

Hello, God's Fabulous People,

Words cannot express the joy I feel in sharing my heart, testimony, story, and faith with you. When God first spoke to me about writing a book, I was thrown off because I was oblivious to the writing process. I immediately started thinking about my lack of education, status, and spiritual development. I mean, who would care about the tragedies of my life. In my mind, I was a broken little girl walking around in a woman's body, acting like I had my ish to together, but man, it was all a front. I wish I could articulate the energy it took to put on for other people who were probably just as jacked up like me. But each day, I was blessed with breath in my body—I was determined to make that day count, and each one He blessed me with after that. Nothing about my life has been simple. It has been downright hard, but as I was crawling through the trenches of life, God was crawling with me. Man, He has been there for every mistake, downfall, horrible decision, wrong relationships, abandonment, people hurt, and every other crazy thing I encountered. Quite naturally, I did not see this during the storm because it was raining and cloudy, but now that the storms passed, I can see clearly. When I complained about being alone and having to tackle the world on my own–He was there. So, I had to repent for my lack of understanding regarding His constant presence in my life. The word says we perish for lack of knowledge, and I was perishing but blaming it on my mother, father, environment, the hood, culture, and the world. It was everybody's fault but mine. One day I took a long hard look in the mirror and realized just how long I had been pouting, and nothing was changing, so I had to BOSS UP. When we hear the term BOSS UP, we immediately think about a job, career, money, material possessions, and status. No sir, I had to BOSS UP in the SPIRIT. You see, I kept warring in the flesh, but the true struggle was in the spirit. As a child, I watched my mother cry out to God during the weakest moments of her life, and I did not understand as a child, but it finally dawned on me one day. She was on to something. I was so busy judging her faults that I could not see that God looks past the faults and sees the needs when we cry out to Him. You see, a man looks at the outward appearance, but God looks at the heart. We look at the designer labels, the subdivision others live in, the car they drive, and the people by whom they are surrounded. God looks at the heart riddled with pain, rejection, bitterness, regret, loneliness, people-pleasing, pride, lust, and all that other junk that we bury and try to act like it is dead. During the writing process, God revealed to me that His glory is always present in ALL things.

What the enemy meant for bad, God will use it for Him to be lifted so that others can be drawn to Him. No matter what you are facing now or in the past, God is being gloried in your life if you are still breathing and pushing through. As I prepare to share **My Story**, open your heart, and allow **God's Glory** to rest in and upon you. The key to success is yielding to God and giving Him permission to lead and guide you even in your mess. He is waiting for you to COME AS YOU ARE!

Chapter One
It's Story Time

"And you will know the truth, and the truth will set you free." John 8:32

Do you remember Storytime? Whether it was in kindergarten when the teacher gathered the students to read the lines of a colorful book filled with pictures to peak your childlike imaginations. Or maybe you had the mother or father who enjoyed reading or making up stories before bedtime. I hope it is safe to say that everyone loves a good story.

Everyone has a story to tell. It does not matter whether it is their story or someone else's. We, as a human race, love to talk and share. Well, I have a story to tell, but brace yourself because this story is ALL about me—

the good, the bad, the ugly, the sad, the regrets, the mistakes, the spiritual warfare, the triumphs, and the victories. You see, life is full of ups and downs, but I learned to trust the process. At first, I trusted in man's process. I followed the status quo by going along to get along, but people kept changing on me. God, on the other hand, remained the same.

I struggled! Let me repeat, your girl struggled! People look at me today and swear I had an easy life, but I can honestly say sometimes it felt like I was experiencing hell on earth. Every day is not supposed to be peaches and cream, but Lord, I do not think I was catching any breaks. I had to take control of my life and consciously choose for it to be better.

If you did not know, choosing life or death, blessing, or cursing, is your God-given right. *Deuteronomy 30:19 says, "I call heaven and earth to record this day against you, that I have set before you **life and death, blessing and cursing:** therefore, **choose life,** that **both thou and thy seed may live.**"*

You have been given the power to choose, and life has taught me that many choose based on emotions and not the truth of God's word. Making emotional choices creates open doors for the enemy to wreak havoc in your life. I was always emotional about something, and it was evident based on the condition of my life.

God ain't (yes, I know ain't is not proper English) playing games with His people! Heaven and earth are recording the option you choose that is set before you every day. You can choose to live, which will spring forth blessings or die, manifesting either spiritual or natural death. Either way, something will manifest, and the manifestation does not only affect you but your seeds (kids).

See, that is the one thing I had to think long and hard about. Did I want my mistakes and hindrances to affect the lives of my children? We often fail to consider generational curses and their adverse effects when left unhandled. Life is hard when the ones before you fail to teach you God's truth versus the world's truth. I had to learn to navigate through life the hard way. I was left to fend for myself because my parents were dealing with life-on-life terms. My mother and father were dealing with issues from their childhoods when I became an added addition to their previous life struggles.

It almost makes you wonder why God would allow children to be born to men and women who are broken, rejected, wounded, and traumatized themselves. I mean, He knows ALL things, so why not let the parent(s) get their life in order and then send the children. Doesn't this make logical sense?

Yes, to the human mind, but He said, "Sam, My ways are not your ways, and My thoughts are not your thoughts." When I became a parent, this made so much sense, and that is when I fully understood that His grace is sufficient in all things, and He knows what He is doing.

So, with, life and the challenges that came with it forced me to become the character in a story filled with shocking details. My life is far from a fairy tale based on make-believe. Every detail has helped shape and mold my life, but had it been up to me, I would have changed the narrative to fit my grand expectations. The scenes of my story would exhibit constant acts of love, laughter, lavish gifts, romance, peace, beauty, the perfect man, a fat bank account, and so much more.

The real-life story consists of hurt, pain, rejection, abuse, sickness, parental abandonment, trauma, disappointment, regrets, addiction, and plenty of mistakes. Oh, but when I chose to relinquish control to God, He began changing the narrative of **My Story to reveal His Glory**!

You can attempt to lay claim on your lives as if they are your own, but let me warn you, this is a lie from the pits of hell. You belong to God, and when you learn how to serve Him with your whole heart, you begin to see Him move in ways beyond your imagination.

When people look at me, they ASSUME I am in perfect health, and my life is fabulous, and it is, but do not think for a moment that I am not battling with something or someone. I struggle just like everybody else. Yet, I have learned how to turn my negatives into positives. You see, the way I grew up, I had to turn my frowns into smiles if I wanted to survive.

Don't ever judge a book by its cover because you will never know the true content unless you read the story. Contrary to popular belief, I battle day in and day out because I suffer in my body, which I will discuss in another chapter. You and I were created with a purpose. My purpose in this season is to share my story and to encourage others through my testimony.

Most importantly, I am amplifying my voice and advocating for the miraculous glory of God. My brothers and sisters, the blood still works, and the Holy Spirit is always ready and willing to lead, guide and direct you towards your God-given destiny and purpose.

My Story, God's Glory, will help you take a closer look at your story to see the hand of God and where He has brought you from versus where He is taking you to.

Chapter Two
A Weak Foundation

"You can't build a great building on a weak foundation." Gordon B. Hinckley

I have no idea how I made it except by the mercy and grace of God. The enemy or the destroyer had a smooth hatred for me, and I could not figure out why for several years. I spent so much time thinking I was cursed, or God hated me because my life was so broken and full of trauma.

I am not the only one who has felt as if life was full of lemons, with no possible way of making lemonade. I get so tired of hearing people talk about taking the lemons of life and making lemonade. Well, what happens when you do not have all the ingredients? Nothing! You find yourself stuck where you started—still holding the lemons. It is mind-blowing if you ask me. We are born into this world to face trouble immediately. If the enemy does not kill you in the womb, his ultimate plan is to keep at it until his mission is accomplished throughout the course of your life.

I am a living witness to this fact. Your divine purpose is a **threat** to the enemy. Let's look at Jesus as an example. He was barely born when the king put out orders to kill every male child under the age of two. Why? He heard about the coming of a child who would become King of Kings and Lord and Lords! Which meant in his mind he would no longer be relevant without realizing Jesus still had to grow up.

The enemy has heard about you, and he is willing to do anything to stop you from becoming relevant in the kingdom of God. There is nothing new under the sun. The enemy is still sending out orders to kill innocent children before they can come into the full knowledge of who they are in Christ. In this day and time, orders come through molestation, abortions, abuse, abandonment, rejection, and much more. If he cannot kill physically, he will do it spiritually, mentally, emotionally, and financially.

Before I entered the birth canal to come into this cruel world, I was attacked. As I lay comfortably nestled in my mother's womb, she was battling with some personal demons. I was subjected to things no newborn child should ever have to experience.

The anticipation of new life is looked upon as an honor in the real world. But what about an unrealistic world tainted with pain, darkness, brokenness, fear, rejection, and dysfunction. What about the parent who is lost and totally disconnected from life? In most cases, the father is disconnected because they do not understand the bond between the mother and the unborn child.

Unfortunately, in my case, the disconnect was with the one who carried me in her womb for nine months battling with nausea, vomiting, a protruding belly, cramping, swollen feet, and sleepless nights. She endured the grueling nine months of pregnancy symptoms while battling heroin addiction.

Even amid my mother's addiction, God shielded me because He had other plans for my life. She could have easily aborted me, or I could have died during one of her episodes, but God had great need of me. The day my mother went into labor, she was shooting heroin and drinking codeine (syrup) or what the streets like to call "purple stuff or lean." As a result of her drug binge, I had to stay in the NICU for two months to detox the drugs in my system after delivery.

Fetal exposure to drugs is a growing epidemic that is affecting both mothers and children. Recent data suggest that nearly twenty-five million Americans aged 12 or older are current illicit drug users; this estimate represents 9.2 percent of the population. Illicit drugs include marijuana/hashish, cocaine (including crack), heroin, hallucinogens, inhalants, or prescription-type psychotherapeutics used non-medically.

As sad as it may sound, my mother, who had me at twenty-five, was taught to use heroin from her parents. Usually, these are bad habits you learn in the street, but not in my family. I can only imagine the thoughts rambling through her head or the pain she must have felt even to consider harming herself and her body in this way at such a youthful age. To think her parents were the ones to influence her is insane, but one dysfunction always connects or leads to another, and this was dysfunction at the highest level.

My family dynamic was built on a weak foundation. A foundation that should have been built on the Chief Cornerstone (Jesus) was built on pain, poverty, problems, and self-pity. The dysfunction of my bloodline consisted of drug addiction, physical, mental, verbal, emotional, financial, and spiritual abuse.

Strongholds and demonic cycles exposed themselves in each generation. My grandmother used drugs; therefore, my mother used drugs. My father physically abused my mother, but her father abused her mother. Then I experienced abuse of different sorts in certain relationships throughout my life.

The enemy has a way of making cycles continue from generation to generation through open doors that we often fail to recognize and close. I never met my grandfather, but whatever my grandmother experienced in life, either with or before him, made her turn to pain meds for relief. The emotional struggle for the women in my life has been real. Pain will make you do and accept some crazy things.

My mother and father were at each other's throat's day and night. All they did was fuss and fight. I do not recall a time when they were loving and caring towards one another. Since I was a little girl, I could only assume the disconnect was due to my mother's drug addiction that eventually escalated from heroin to crack. If you have never dealt with an addict, it is tough and disheartening to see, especially for someone you genuinely love.

Do not get me wrong. I believe my mother would have been a perfect parent without the influence of drugs. My father, on the other hand, was everything to me. He embraced me as his little princess. I always felt unique and protected when I was around him. I loved him with every fiber of my being, and he loved me. I can recall long days and nights riding in the passenger seat of my father's taxi. He drove taxis for a living, and I spent more time with him than with my mother. He was so patient, gentle, and kind to me.

All I wanted as a child was a happy home. A place I could call my own and not feel inadequate or insecure. Watching my mother battle caused a mountain of insecurities in my life. I was willing to do anything to make her happy, hoping she would stop the drugs and stay home with me. Nothing I did or said was ever good enough.

Eventually, I wrapped my mind around the fact that if I did not have my mother's attention, at least I had my father. I mean, some kids did not have one or the other. I was taught to pray at a very early age. So, I decided to pray that my mother would get better one day, and we could all be one happy family. My father was always there. We just needed my mother, his wife, and life would be good, or so I thought.

My father became extremely ill when he was only sixty years old and was tragically taken from me at twelve. My world was already turned upside down but losing him was an even devastating blow to any hope I had for a bright future.

How could God take the stable parent and leave me with the unstable one? My mind was warped! My dad was not perfect, but he made me a priority. Saying goodbye to him was the hardest thing I ever faced in life. If I could see him one more time, I would ask him why he had to leave so soon. Only God truly knows the answer but knowing why may have eased the pain in my carnal mind even though my heart was broken.

    I really did not come to grips with the loss of my father until life started happening to me. There were many days I wished I were with him and not living in this cold, cruel world. Pain will cause you to check out on yourself, and if you are not available for yourself, you cannot be available for anyone else. After my fathers' death, my mother checked out even more. I was like the kid in the movie "Home Alone," doing what I wanted to do, when I wanted to do it, and how I wanted to do it.

    Life is all about learning lessons. I was so angry with my mother growing up because I did not understand her struggle. I was much older when I realized that drugs help people to escape their present reality. I made it about me, but the issues were constantly evolving within her. My mother was aware of her inner demons, and she fought like hell to defeat them. There were times when she won and got herself cleaned up, but those demons always found a way back in to win over her.

As a little girl, I would often hear my mother crying, praying, and screaming out to God the following day after being out the whole night doing drugs. Hearing her repenting and praying while on her knees really irritated my soul. How could she get high all night and then cry out to God for repentance the next day, yet go out and do it all over again?

Why not just stop? Why keep hurting yourself repeatedly and then expect God to save you? I was a kid, but even I had this much sense. She would pray and read her bible aloud like clockwork every time. Her flesh was in constant war with her spirit. The Apostle Paul said his spirit was always willing, but his flesh was weak. He said I know to do good, but evil is always present.

Well, I can say for sure until this day, God has kept her, and He has definitely looked out for me, so her prayers still packed power. This may seem confusing to some self-righteous folks, but God encourages us to *come as we are*. Man looks on the outer parts, but He looks at the heart. My mother was not a bad person. God chose one path for her, but life took her on a different journey. I love the GPS because if you choose to take a different route other than what is instructed, the word "rerouting" will pop up and get you back on course.

One thing I can say about God is He is no respecter of a person. Many are bound because they are waiting for God to automatically reroute them when they must take steps to surrender their will first. The word tells us faith without works is dead. You may not have the willpower to stop and surrender everything overnight, but effort is necessary. You must be willing to relinquish your ways to the Almighty God, letting Him know you desire to be cleansed, healed, delivered, and set free.

Despite my mother's strongholds, she was serious about her relationship with God. His grace covered her all these years. He honored her prayers even in protecting me throughout my life.

My mother battled addiction on and off for almost fifteen years. The time came when she totally surrendered her will to the will of her Father, and He healed her. After getting cleaned, she went back to school to obtain her degree as a substance abuse counselor. She allowed her war wounds to become life for those who were dying in their addictions. My mother could have died in the streets, but God's grace provided a way of escape, and His glory manifested through those she was able to reach.

My mother always proclaimed that hell was real and not a place anyone wanted to visit. She could share this as a relative truth because she knew what it felt like to live in hell on earth. Her addiction caused her to be mentally, emotionally, financially, spiritually, and physically controlled by a substance that helped her to escape the realities of life. But

God kept her when the enemy was slowly trying to destroy her.

I wanted to know the God she was crying out to. I wanted my own pain and sorrow to fade away. So as a little girl, I would wait until she left for the day and then sneak into her room to her bible. Then I would find a quiet place to sit and read the words. As I turned the pages, I found nothing but indescribable inner peace.

My revelation of the word was on a child's level, but I felt drawn to God in my heart. The words lit up my life, and I felt a sense of security, much like when my father was alive. As an adult, I see that my destiny was delayed but never denied. Often, we blame others for the mishaps in our lives when they could very well be part of the journey.

God had a plan for my life, and my mother and father were only the vessels He chose to get me into the earth. Yes, I was broken and battling with feeling unwanted, rejected, unloved, thrown away, and abandoned, which is a lot for a kid to bear on her own, but I kept fighting even without knowing the opponent.

    I did not want my father's absence or my mother's addiction to dictate or define my life. But eventually, I started looking for my own ways to escape, which only dug deeper holes for me to fall in.

Chapter Three
Saved By Grace

No weapon formed against you shall prosper.
Isaiah 54:17

No matter where I went, I was not accepted. I did not seem to fit in anywhere. In the seventh grade, the kids constantly bullied me because I was either too light-skinned or too skinny. Let's not forget I was still having issues fitting in at home. My mother and I could not seem to connect at all, even after the passing of my father. Quite naturally, my feelings of rejection and insecurities pushed me into people-pleasing mode.

I started doing any and everything to be part of the in-crowd. There was a deep dark void in the pit of my soul that I was never able to articulate into words. I had an itch that could never be scratched. I sympathized with my mother because I caught a glimpse of her life and how it felt to want peace and not be able to find it. Pain will lead you down some dark valleys.

I did what most kids my age do. I found a group and stuck with them. Now that I think about it, I was trying to create a place to feel wanted and loved. I started hanging with this group of girls, who, in time, began to bully and taunt me while pretending to be my friends. All I wanted to do was feel like I belonged somewhere, anywhere.

Trying to fit in became my new norm, but I have always been the oddball in the group, even into adulthood. I spent most of my natural life surviving and figuring things out on my own through the grace of God. He has been with me every step of the way, even in my mistakes. I am grateful He never forsook me even though I had to grow up faster than I anticipated.

Seeing the world through the eyes of a child is amazing because everything appears to be pure and innocent. I mean, children are incredibly open and optimistic about everything. Many are not afraid to take a risk or be adventurous until something or someone changes this perception for them. I was one of those bright-eyed, enthusiastic little girls until my life took a drastic turn.

It was a regular day like any other when these two guys from the neighborhood approached me. I did not feel threatened because I knew them. They asked me if I wanted to hang out, and of course, I said yes. I jumped in the car with them, and we headed to the corner store. They grabbed some beers and asked if I wanted one. I kindly declined, but they purchased it anyway.

Again, the people-pleasing spirit kicked in, and when we returned to the vehicle, one of the guys asked me once more if I wanted the beer. Everything in me was screaming no, but when I opened my mouth, what rolled off my tongue was yes. The guy handed me the beer, and I must admit it was the nastiest beverage I ever tasted. I did not want to appear weak and immature, so I gulped it down as fast as possible.

Man, the joys of peer pressure taught me a valuable lesson that day. My alcohol tolerance was extremely low. I was tipsy in no time. While I was tagging along for the ride, they never mentioned where we were going. I do not even remember if I asked. The beer started taking its course, and before long, I was in the backseat feeling all giggly and silly.

The driver continued driving to a park near the bayou. I was looking around, thinking we pulled into the park to chill, but they had a motive from the moment they laid eyes on me. One of them instructed me to get out of the car. I followed the instructions, still not putting the pieces together.

I was drunk, but not enough to recognize I was in danger. As I stood on the side of the car, I overheard them discussing their plan to rape and kill me. One of the guys had a gun. Lord, how was I going to get out of this? Why did I even get in the car in the first place? God, why me? These questions bombarded me while I stood there, trying not to panic and make matters worse.

It was apparent that neither one of them knew what they wanted because they kept arguing. I felt like I was watching my mother and father all over again. They could not decide who would initiate the rape and then finish by shooting me. My body became numb as I stood there waiting for them to decide. I mean, life was not going in my favor. My father was dead, and my mother was on drugs. Maybe this was God's way of taking me out of my misery or letting me be with my father again.

When they stopped fighting, one of the guys walked towards me, and I saw my whole life flash before my eyes. I opened my mouth, and I started to plead. I begged them not to hurt me, and I yelled out I was on my cycle. They stopped and stared at each other for a minute. One of the perpetrators held me down to search me and found that I was telling the truth.

As much as I hated being on my cycle, this was one time I was super excited. They both became angry and frustrated before telling me to get back into the car. I was unaware of the next destination, but I was still alive. Just think I knew them from the hood and could identify them to the police. That alone was reason enough to shoot me and then leave me to die in that park.

I sat in that back seat, trying to think of a plan to escape. If I opened the door and jumped out, I could still get run over by a car and die. Yelling was not going to help because they had a gun and could shoot me in the backseat and hide the body. My heart was pounding so hard I thought I was having a heart attack. Once they realized I was more of a liability than an asset, I guess I had to go by any means necessary. The driver was driving about thirty miles when he exited the freeway.

The passenger opened the door and pushed me out of the moving vehicle. I was screaming and rolling in the street, thinking that my life was about to end. There was not a car in sight. Once again, God protected me.

I was in a state of shock, but I managed to get up, shaken, afraid, and still drunk. I have been shaking off trauma and getting back up my whole life when I think about it. I started walking, not sure where I was going or what I was about to do. We did not have cell phones back then, so I needed help. I stumbled into these apartments and started knocking on random doors.

Finally, a door opened, and these two teenagers invited me in. They did not ask very many questions. I guess the look on my face said enough. I remember falling asleep on their floor until I was awakened to screaming adults. When their parents arrived, I can only imagine the shock of finding a total stranger sleeping on their floor.

As a parent, I would have reacted the same way, but I was so grateful that God used those two teens as angels to assist me that day. I got up, and I left walking to a nearby Whataburger, hoping to find someone to hitch a ride with.

Yes, I hear you thinking! I was almost raped and killed in the last car I jumped in, and there I was about to do it again. Well, what other options did I have? This man saw me and asked if I was okay. I told him I needed to get home, and he offered to give me a ride. I prayed the whole time I was in the car. I had no clue who this man was, but he was angel number three sent by God to save me that day.

The enemy is crafty and cunning. These two guys were sent on assignment as wolves in sheep's clothing. What I saw as innocent was a plot for the enemy to destroy me that day—but God! I was looking through the lenses of optimism when I should have been screaming stranger danger. Again, they were familiar, so I assumed no harm, no foul.

I was so excited to make it home. I walked into the house and went straight to my room. All I could do was sit and reflect on the fact that I could have been left for dead in a park. This incident changed my perception of life and people.

I kept this incident to myself. But I also became introverted and unable to trust people very much after this. Isn't it funny how one bad incident can hinder every area of your life? Fear is the number one tactic used by the enemy to keep you mentally and emotionally imprisoned. As much as I hoped this isolated incident would be the last of my sorrows, there were many more to come. But I was grateful for the fact that God showed me at twelve years old that He was with me and nothing the enemy did could take me out.

Genesis 50:20 says, "You intended to harm me, but God intended it for good to accomplish what is now being done, the saving of many lives."

This passage of scripture shows Joseph's response to his brothers who attempted to kill him, but God intervened, and he was sold into slavery. After being sold into slavery, he found favor with the king but was falsely accused by the king's wife of rape. This false accusation cost him fourteen years of his life in prison, but God had a plan. He was released from prison and promoted to second in command under the king. God positioned him to save the same people from famine and death who tried to kill him.

Nothing you have been through will be wasted. God is going to use everything in your life to bring Him glory. Years later, I was working as a cashier at Foodarama. By this time, I had given my life to the Lord. I looked up, and the two guys who intended to rape and kill me were standing in my line. I could not forget their faces if I wanted to. At that moment, my heart sank, and the gruesome memories flooded my mind. All I remember thinking is God forgave me, so I must forgive them!

One of the guys recognized me and immediately began to apologize for his actions and the actions of his friend. I was able to look him in his eyes and tell him I forgive them both. I could have easily acted out of character and rehashed what they did and how it made me feel, but for what? What would it prove? What would it change? I was alive and well. I did not say I was not wounded, or the memory never popped up here and there, but God saved me from the grips of the enemy.

I realized what they did to me could have been weighing them down and stopping them from progressing in life, so like Joseph, I was able to help save and release them from inner bondage and turmoil. There are few words to describe how I felt at that moment. Having the power to release love versus hate meant the world to me. I have always been a feisty firecracker, but feisty becomes gentle when God begins doing a new work in you. The word says, "With love and kindness have I drawn thee!"

This is one of the many incidents God used and is still using to shape my life. As you journey through the remainder of my story, you will find that God is faithful, even when you are not. You will find that He is an ever-present help in the time of trouble. You might relate to several of my incidents but relating and responding are two different things.

Life has taught me to respond based on God's truth versus my emotions. Facts are just what they are—facts! Emotions, on the other hand, are subject to change at any time. I wasted a lot of time on an emotional roller coaster, but I finally decided to exit the ride that was going nowhere fast. I am not alive today because I want to be. I am alive today because GRACE saved me. My trauma sent me down a path of destruction, but God's truth redirected my course, and because of Him, I live!

Chapter Four
Underdeveloped

Thus says the LORD: "Cursed is the man who trusts in man and makes flesh his strength, whose heart turns away from the LORD.
Jeremiah 17:5 (ESV)

Wounds tend to bleed, especially when they are not allowed to breathe and properly heal. The wounds I sustained during my adolescent and teen years became infected. A temporary scab grew over the scars, but eventually, I found some way to peel them off and make them bleed again. Even though I was wounded, I was determined not to use drugs as a coping mechanism.

I had every reason to follow a familiar path. Witnessing the gruesome effect drugs had on my mother and how they destroyed everything connected to her, I found other ways to cope with life. I dodged the addiction to street drugs, but I learned to cope with something just as potent–the opposite sex! Since my mother was doing her, I had little supervision or structure. Around the age of fourteen, I was struggling with everything from identity to rejection. Do you have any idea how hard it is to be a teenager without guidance? I had a vivid imagination, and I was not afraid to act out anything that came to mind.

By this time, my father had been gone about two years, and not having his presence did a number on my morale. He treated me like a princess, and I held on to that, thinking all young boys and men would do the same. Unfortunately, this was not the case, at least in my life. Broken people attract other broken people. Life would be so much easier if the brokenness were evident from first glance or conversation.

I met boys who appeared to be cool but only wanted one thing, and that was sex. They were not trying to get to know me for me, and this was frustrating. I was dealing with hell at home and needed someone who would understand. Do not get me wrong, they listened, but long enough to interject their needs over mine.

Again, more wolves presented themselves in sheep's clothing, and I was the prey. I was never taught what to look for in a boyfriend. What was I supposed to expect from him? Would we one day fall in love? Did I have to have sex to be accepted? These were unanswered questions I learned through experience.

My focus should have been on school, but I lacked motivation. My mother was not necessarily concerned about my educational future. I was in the world creating my own moves. The feelings of worthlessness started to smother me, so I started searching for an alternative route.

Sitting in a classroom listening to a teacher was not helping me with the thoughts rambling through my mind. I could not hear anyone for the voice of the enemy telling me I was nothing and would never be anything. So, I ran from the classroom into the streets.

When I was in the seventh grade, I started skipping school every day. I did not want to be there, and more than anything, I tried to avoid being bullied. My focus shifted from books to boys. If a boy was cute and showed interest, that was more than enough to consider dating or having sex because I needed to feel like I mattered to someone.

My mother was not checking for report cards or attending parent-teacher conferences. I was fending for myself. As far as she knew, I was going to school every day. I started dating this guy who was seventeen years old. We started having sex, and in time, I found out I was pregnant.

To say I was petrified is an understatement. I was barely taking care of myself, and now I had to be responsible for another human being. I was fourteen years old, and even though I was no longer fourteen in my body, I was still fourteen in my mind. Which meant I was very immature.

Carrying a child in my belly for nine months as a little girl was rough. The looks and stares when I went places were frustrating. Not being able to play and be a typical teen was even more irritating. Let's not talk about the morning sickness, cramps, constant hunger, and mood swings. My belly was huge compared to my frail petite frame.

Thankfully, my mother and her boyfriend stepped in to assist me. When I found out I was pregnant, I made one of the worse decisions of my life. I decided to drop out of school. I was not prepared to deal with the hustle and bustle of trying to raise a child and go to school. After experiencing the bumpy roads, I traveled, I was not about to trust anyone with my child.

I anticipated so many things throughout the pregnancy, but nothing prepared me for the actual birthing experience. Man, I felt like I was being ripped from the inside out. I was blessed to birth a healthy baby boy. The idea of being a mother seemed so unreal. I was needing my mother, but now this innocent child needed me to be his mother. God has a funny sense of humor.

I was excited but scared as hell because this was not a doll that I could get tired of and toss in the corner. He always required my undivided attention. I enjoyed being in the hospital because the nurses did most of the work, but it was all on me when we got home. His father tried to be there for us but did something stupid and ended up in prison.

Getting pregnant early was hard enough, but not having the child's father around was even harder. The feelings of losing my father resurfaced all over again. I did not want my son to face the same dilemmas of being a fatherless child, but apparently, this was out of my control.

I loved my little man based on what I knew love to be. My love for him forced me to ensure I never intentionally put him in harm's way or made him feel like he was not loved or protected. Even though I dropped out of school, I knew my next move had to be my best move. I started working and doing the best I could to provide for both of us. He became my top priority but keep in mind getting pregnant does not change the condition of your life; it just adds another person to it. I was still seeking and searching for love in all the wrong places.

The voids in my life were still empty, so I continued falling for the wolves in sheep's clothing—the brothers with the conversation to entice a female to do just about anything. I was doing anything all right. Giving up my body to feel whole made perfect sense when I was doing it, but today I understand I was underdeveloped and had no idea of the negative impact on my body and soul.

Soul ties are real and can become extremely dangerous, especially when you have no idea they exist. I was never taught about protecting my soul and becoming one in body and spirit, which means you take on the individuals' characteristics and issues if they have some. I would have become a nun had I known this because I crossed paths with some treacherous fellows.

You must be careful who you connect with because your demons become their demons and vice versa. Then if you have children, the poor child has to battle with both sets of dysfunctions. My kids were halfway grown when I received this revelation.

Yes, you read that right, kids meaning more than one. When I turned eighteen, I became pregnant with my second child. At this point, I was in full-blown survival mode. I was no longer considered a little girl since I chose to do adult things. I guess this is why the seasoned saints always said, "A child should stay in a child's place!"

When teen girls my age were looking for prom dresses, I was looking for pampers and formula. When they were preparing to graduate from high school, I graduated into adulthood as a mother with two boys. College was nowhere in my future. I was a seventh-grade dropout with two kids by eighteen. And once again, the child's father was not present in his life, but God had a ram in the bush this time.

I met this guy six months after giving birth to my son. He appeared to be pretty leveled headed and was not turned off by the fact that I had two kids. We dated for a little while, and everything was going well when I found out I was pregnant with baby number three.

At the tender age of nineteen, I was a mother to five children (he already had two kids). He wanted to do the right thing by making us an official family, so he asked me to marry him, and I said yes. Did I have any other options? I loved him, but I often wondered if I was ready to settle down and be a wife. I watched my mother and grandmother live miserable lives with their husbands, and that was one cycle I did not want to repeat.

We got married a year after giving birth to yet another son. I was popping out babies left and right. But as I stated in a previous chapter, we were not mentally or emotionally prepared for such a huge responsibility. As they say in the streets, "We had to fake it, just to make it!" We both lacked in many areas, but we pulled together to make the household work as best as possible.

God chose us to bring these kids into the world, which means He saw something in us that we did not see in ourselves. I guess this is why He trusted us to steward another one of His precious gifts when I became pregnant with our last and final child. After five boys, He finally blessed us with a daughter. Having a girl in the house was terrific because I was overwhelmed with all the male testosterones.

I counted myself as underdeveloped, but God said, "I will not put more on you than you can handle." Only God gives life; therefore, according to Him, I was able to handle being a mother. Did I know everything I needed to know? Of course not! But the Holy Spirit stepped in to teach me what I needed to know. When I made mistakes, He took up the slack and showed me where I went wrong. He is still teaching me to this day!

Chapter Five
Trusting In The Lord

Trust in the LORD with all your heart and lean not on your own understanding.
Proverbs 3:5

Marriage is a huge responsibility. What on God's green earth was I thinking? From fourteen to nineteen my life was consumed with children, then I dared to enter a binding covenant relationship. I was married with children, yet still a child myself. I missed out on so many things.

I mean, I missed exploring the simple things in life. Every path I traveled on was hard and rugged. It was like I had to do everything the hard way. I know this may sound crazy, but I would have probably rejected anything that came to me without struggle during that time. Marriage appears to be easy in the beginning, but over time it gets complicated. The couple is happy and loving the first year, but that love turns to hate and happiness to depression. Watching my parents' marriage should have been enough to get me together before including someone else, but I convinced myself that I would be better and do better than them.

This sounded wonderful, but I did not have the blueprint for better. I had no idea what better looked like because all I ever saw was misery, pain, division, and brokenness.

We had six kids depending on us to get this right. As parents, we were accountable for their mental, spiritual, and emotional well-being. So, we decided to do something different. My husband and I started attending church, my uncles' church to be exact. I was so excited!

Things began to shift when we decided to include God in our lives, hearts, and home. The blood of Jesus covered all the darkness I encountered, and His marvelous light was shining in my life. I learned so much about God. He taught me how to be a woman, a mother, a wife, and a daughter who pleased Him and not a man. All the things I longed for and needed were being revealed to me through the word of God. I desperately sought God for a do-over.

I thought I knew God based on what I saw my mother do growing up, but I was finally learning Him for myself, and the feeling was incredible. When you genuinely seek God, He will not leave you ignorant of satan's devices. During the final phases of the writing process, God was still revealing truths of how His glory carried me throughout my life.

He reminded me of how my mother would binge on crack all night but be on her face crying out to Him for mercy the following day. I did not understand it. Hearing her pray would irritate my soul, but God revealed that I would not have known how to seek Him for myself if she did not set the example of prayer. My God!

Even in her state of addiction, she was still training me in the way I should go, and I was so focused on her flaws that I could not see the grace of God upon her life. You must catch this in the spirit! I stated in Samantha's letter, "COME AS YOU ARE!" We miss the glory of God because WE try to come a certain way, but He wants us just as we are—jacked up, cracked up, sexed-up, drugged up, and every other up you can think of.

I honor my mother today because she took what she had and used it to the best of her ability. God gave her just enough to set me on the path that HE designated for my life. I spent a lot of time wishing my life had been different, but the storyline played out the way God intended. I may have caused some alterations to the plans along the way, but even in that, God has been faithful to use everything the enemy meant for evil, for Him to be glorified.

God was showing up and showing out in my life. I had a seventh-grade education, but I worked in corporate America as if I had a diploma and a college degree. People have always been intrigued with my personality and how I carry myself. God's glory was resting upon me, but I did not understand this then. I worked my butt off because I wanted to provide a better life for my children.

During the marriage, I worked at a credit union, and I fixed hair on the weekends. I worked for a temporary agency while waiting to get on permanent. My mind was made up that if I did not get on permanent, I would enroll in beauty school and pursue hair as a career. I did not get hired as I anticipated, so in 2010 I enrolled in beauty school.

My husband took on a second job to support the household. I was blessed with great mentors who took me under their wings and carried me through the entire journey. I started assisting Patric and Kay, and they taught me everything I needed to know about hair. I started traveling and taking courses on my own because I was hungry for knowledge.

I was not about to perish because I was too lazy to learn and hone in on the gift God was presenting to me. The word says, "Your gifts will make room for you and put you before great men." I watched this scripture unfold in my life. The more I sought Him, the more doors were opened onto me.

Now let me be clear when I say God was doing remarkable things in my life, but the fiery attacks of the enemy were still coming. Only this time, he was coming in ways I would have never imagined. I was being persecuted in the church. Can you believe this? The one place where I finally found some solace was turning into a warzone. The warfare was so bad it started affecting my marriage and keep in mind this is my uncle's church—not a play uncle, but my mother's brother.

I will go into greater detail about him in the next chapter, but the spirit of control was on him so bad that he put me out of the church in 2006. Yes, you read that right. My own uncle booted me out of the church because I was not afraid to call him on his mess. He described it as being rebellious against authority. He was absolutely correct because I was following the authority of the Holy Spirit when he wanted me to bow to him.

Man, look, I heard about Jim Jones, and I was not about to drink the Kool-Aid in the name of the Lord. I will admit I have done some crazy things in my life. I am far from perfect, but my spirit man was stirring and not in a good way. When he booted me out of the church, he told my husband he could not talk to or help me. Now where they do that at! When God specifically said, "What I have put together, let no man put asunder!"

He was operating under demonic spirits of control, manipulation, and witchcraft. My husband was stuck for a little while, but again the glory of God manifested on my behalf, and God broke that demonic hold. He finally left, and we started attending another church. Oh, the enemy tried it, but God.

During this encounter, Proverbs, 3:5-6 became the foundation I stood on. I had no other choice but to trust in the Lord with ALL my heart and lean not to my understanding. Dealing with this type of hurt and betrayal forced me to ACKNOWLEDGE my Father in ALL His ways so that He could direct my path. My uncle had everybody fooled, even me, in the beginning, but God exposed him. Why He chose me, only He knows the real reason.

If I had to give my opinion, I would say it is because He built me little in physical stature but mighty and strong in the spirit. God knew I was going to call my uncles mess to the carpet and not back down. As He was knitting and molding me in my mother's womb, He added these attributes to my life.

The enemy thought he would kill me because of the drugs in my mother's system, but God said, "No, she is mine!" Send her to the NICU to be detoxed in the flesh because I have fortified her in the spirit, and she shall LIVE and be a voice for the voiceless!

Chapter Six
Beware Of The Cult

"I appeal to you, brothers, to watch out for those who cause divisions and create obstacles contrary to the doctrine that you have been taught; avoid them. For such persons do not serve our Lord Christ, but their own appetites, and by smooth talk and flattery, they deceive the hearts of the naive." Romans 16:17-18

In the last chapter, I briefly discussed the tragedy I experienced at my uncle's church. I want to share the experience because I believe it will help someone today. There are so many people sitting under the leadership of false prophets and controlling witches calling it a work of the Lord.

It is heartbreaking to fathom the amount of damage these spirits create within the body of

Christ. Innocent people who just want to love and serve God are being deceived because of greed and status. But what does it profit a man to gain the whole world but lose his soul? Can you put a price tag on your soul? Of course not, because it is not yours to dictate. Your soul belongs to God, and only He has the power to determine where your soul will rest for eternity.

I mentioned the infamous religious cult leader Jim Jones who in the late '70s portrayed himself as a self-proclaimed messiah of the Peoples Temple, leading nine hundred of the members to their death in a mass suicide. Come on, people, God is a just God! He wants us to have abundant life. The enemy is the one who steals, kills, and destroys. Mr. Jones was sent on assignment to destroy the purpose and assignments that those nine hundred people were created to fulfill.

That was Jim Jones but let me introduce you to my uncle and former pastor, Ronald Mitchell. The senior pastor of the Body of

Christ Church in Magnolia, Texas. In 2018 he was sentenced to 75 years in prison for five counts of sexual assault of a child.

Yes, you read that correctly, my friend. The dishonorable Pastor Ronald Mitchell is serving a life sentence for yielding to his flesh and not walking in the spirit. Whatever reaction from the shock you had, multiply it by infinity, and you can imagine my reaction when this dark secret was exposed.

Oh, how I wish I were as mature as I am now in the word to understand and heed the warning in Matthew 7:15 that says, "Beware of false prophets which come to you in sheep's clothing, but inwardly they are ravening wolves."

Or had I understood what Jesus was teaching in Matthew 7:22-23 when He said, "Many will say on that day, 'Lord, Lord, did I not prophesy in your name? Then I will tell them plainly, 'I never knew you. Away from me, you evildoer.'"

The accounts from witnesses and survivors of the Jim Jones religious cult were similar if not identical to the details of what took place with the cult my uncle was running. There was physical abuse, sexual abuse, mental manipulation, and forced isolation from people who were not church members. When I was a member of my uncle's church, I was a young wife. The church provided the privilege of developing friendships with other married couples.

Everything about the Body of Christ Church was amazing. Sunday services and bible study were always on point. One day we were in awe of the mighty move of God, and then suddenly, there was a shift, and the church started to unravel.

My uncle's personality went from charismatic, warm, and inviting to controlling, aggressive, authoritative, and dictating. As his niece, I stayed in constant trouble with "the pastor." I never hesitated to speak up and question the abnormal practices he forced upon the church.

The Apostle Paul told the church to watch out for those who cause divisions and create obstacles contrary to the doctrine that you have been taught because these people did not serve the Lord Christ, but their own appetites, by smooth talk and flattery, to deceive the hearts of the naïve.

We were naïve, all right, and he was definitely flattering us with smooth talk knowing he was deceiving us the whole time. I was incredibly young and had no idea about cults, witchcraft, or the Jezebel spirit. I was always taught the church was where you meet God, get saved, and get healed. But the church is full of so much more, and rightfully so because the church is not the building but the people who enter the building.

I was completely unaware that my uncle was running his church in the same manner as a cult. One of the victims testified to the court that my uncle threatened her. He secured her silence by making her fear death at the hand of God for stopping the movement, as he called it, if she told anyone about their sexual relationship.

I believe her testimony because he also threatened and tried his best to destroy me. After 13 years as a church member, I was kicked out, and he went on a relentless campaign to break up my marriage. That entire moment in history threatened my faith and robbed me entirely of my ability to trust others. I was already struggling in that area from previous incidents in my life.

I never considered that a pastor could have such boldness to represent himself as a man of God, all while unashamedly operating in darkness and evil doings. To add fuel to the fire, he was my blood. Through every situation in my life that I was able to endure up until that point, I endured and overcame by trusting in the God that He preached about.

I became confused about how one keeps trusting in God after traveling through such a dark valley at the hand of a supposed "man of God"? How do I trust people at all in life when most of my life's pain came by way of people? I recall being so wounded and lost because of the events that were contributing to my life story.

Although my faith had been horribly shaken, I did what I knew to do in a time of uncertainty; I cried out to my Heavenly Father. *Our Father in heaven, I do not understand why these strange things have happened to me, so I seek You. Restore my faith Lord, help me trust again for your name's sake.*

An overwhelming amount of life had taken place for me at a rapid pace leaving me shattered and only a fragment of a person. But God has always been faithful to hear my prayers. Daily, God imparted what I needed to keep standing by building me up in wisdom through a personal relationship with Him.

I was still young; therefore, my life journey was far from over. As life carried on and more faith-shattering events took place, I soon realized the hard truth. Everything we experience is preparation for whatever we are destined to face and overcome by trusting wholeheartedly in God.

Sitting under the leadership of Pastor Ronald Mitchell as a member of the Body of Christ Church in Magnolia, Texas, was already written before I was conceived. God predestined me to encounter this journey because it played a significant role in my spiritual development.

It was meant for me to see this type of betrayal up close and personal. God used the foolishness with my uncle to teach me not to fear man. I learned how to amplify my voice to advocate for those who are spiritually weak or depleted.

IT DID NOT FEEL GOOD when I was going through the adversity, persecution, isolation, estrangement from my husband, and total confusion and betrayal. Still, again it was working for my good. My uncle tried to make people think I was crazy and going straight to hell in a handbasket when the whole time it was him with the problem.

I will be honest when I say he scarred me and caused me to doubt my relationship with God. I started second-guessing everything I learned up to that point, and when the enemy started whispering in my ear, contradicting the voice of God, I just shut down.

Nothing was really the same after this. My husband finally left the church, and we went somewhere else, but our marriage was broken. We started dealing with infidelity, and we no longer saw eye to eye as parents. The enemy broke into our home and our marriage and ransacked them both. We allowed him to rob our family because the foundation we built it on was built upon lies, and I believe in my heart that we just did not have the stamina left to recover.

The marriage was officially dead when he put a knife to my throat. During the marriage, he was never abusive, so this was devastating. It was then that I realized the love was gone, or maybe it was never there. But not long after this incident, we got divorced in 2012 after I finished beauty school.

Chapter Seven
Another Hurdle To Cross

I can do all things through him who strengthens me. Philippians 4:13

Okay, so we have discussed abandonment, addiction, loss of a parent, getting thrown from a moving vehicle after potentially getting raped, teen pregnancy, divorce, and a cult. Man, God is good because that is a lot for one little person, but the storms never stop coming. Ecclesiastes says there is a season for everything under the sun.

I had my share of good days, but I was always braced and prepared for the not-so-good days. When I was going through the difficulties of the marriage and dealing with the church hurt, I was hit with yet another obstacle—Crohn's disease!

Crohn's disease is an inflammatory bowel disease that affects the digestive tract. It leads to abdominal pain, severe diarrhea, fatigue, weight loss, and malnutrition. In 2011, I started having severe acid reflux that became unbearable. I went to the doctor, and after running several tests, Crohn's was the cause. It is a rare disease with no known cure, but I know the One who cures all forms of dis-ease.

For the last ten years, I have battled with flare-ups at least twice a year that can last up to two months. Crohn's has affected me mentally, physically, spiritually, financially, socially, and emotionally. Sometimes I feel so alone, but God grants me the strength to endure through every flare-up.

This disease takes a drastic toll on my body, which is why I said in the beginning, "Never judge a book by its cover." I experience weight loss, lack of appetite, vomiting, and severe joint pain when I get sick. I am not able to go anywhere or do much of anything.

Crohn's causes me to be bedridden until it passes.

Now I must interject that this obstacle presented itself when I was finishing beauty school and looking to build my career as a professional stylist. I traveled around the world, learning as much as I could to tame the hair industry. I never wanted a basic salon.

I envisioned an empire, and Crohn's was threatening my vision. For the life of me, I could not figure out why things seemed to happen to me at the most inopportune times.

I was finally doing something positive to build a legacy for my children, and my body was attacked. I was taught never to question God, but I had to ask why. Like every other time, it was for Him to be glorified in my life. Paul had an issue that he called "a thorn in his flesh." He asked God to remove it three times, and His response was, "My grace is sufficient."

If you are battling with anything today, whether physical, spiritual, mental, emotional, or financial, just know that God's grace is sufficient. There have been times in my life when I did not want to hear an encouraging word. I just wanted the pain to end and to be at peace. But the word says there will be trouble in this world, but do not fear because Jesus overcame the world. You are going to deal with life until you take your last breath.

The key to success is dealing with life and not letting life deal with you. I know people who try to escape from life every day. I still try to escape here and there, but there is no escaping what God has predestined for your life. You can run, but you cannot hide. God is omnipresent and has eyes in every place.

After everything I dealt with, getting sick was the last thing I ever imagined happening to me. I put in the sweat and tears to build my business, only to not be as effective because the flare-ups come without warnings. They are never consistent but sporadic, and as a hairstylist, this affects my business.

But with every flare-up, God has always provided and taken great care of my children and me. I have learned to depend on Him for every need. Over the years, I have learned how far I can go before it is time to be still and rest. I know my limitations. I have worked even though I was in pain and weak. Those are the times when I feel God holding me up and sustaining me when my flesh is weak, but my spirit man is strong.

It has not been easy, but I am grateful to be alive. Many do not have the power to fight and or survive, but God has been gracious to me despite me. People are diagnosed with life changes illnesses every day. This is a part of life. But I have learned through my own diagnosis that you can make it through anything if you respond positively.

1st Corinthians 10:13 says, *"No temptation has overtaken you that is not common to man. God is faithful, and He will not let you be tempted beyond your ability, but with the temptation, He will also provide the way of escape, that you may be able to endure it."*

The scripture says God is FAITHFUL. I am a living witness to this fact. No matter what situation or circumstance I have been in, He has always made a way of escape, even for the messes I put myself in. Yes, I have fallen trying to cross some hurdles, but He was there extending His hand to help me up.

We tend to get so down on ourselves that we often fail to give ourselves credit for the small feats. Stop rushing through life and take it one day at a time. Today, I KNOW that I can do ALL things through CHRIST, who gives me strength. I put all my trust in self and in men at one point, but the reward is greater with CHRIST!

Chapter Eight
Still Searching

Blessed is the man that walketh not in the counsel of the ungodly, nor standeth in the way of sinners, nor sitteth in the seat of the scornful. Psalm 1:1

Have you ever wanted something or someone so bad, you were willing to go to any lengths to obtain it or them? Even at the expense of knowing you were treading down the wrong path. I mean, God was sending all kinds of warnings to RUN, but your flesh wanted what it wanted by any means necessary. Okay, maybe I have been the only one to travel down desperation lane in the name of love. I will take full accountability for the not one, not two, not even three but several lapses in judgment over the years.

I was a daddy's girl for the first twelve years of my life. My mind was conditioned to believe that all men should treat you like your Daddy, but this theory proved me wrong. If I had to summarize my past relationships after marriage in three words, I would have to say painful, self-seeking, and tumultuous. For some reason, I entered relationships with the unrealistic expectation that the man would love me, either the same or just as much as I loved them.

Again, this was an unrealistic expectation that set me up for failure every time. Don't you hate how the relationship starts with butterflies and googly eyes but eventually turns to ulcers and rolling eyes with a stiff neck? Why can't the relationship stay consistent from beginning to end? Am I asking for too much, or I was setting the bar too low?

My intentions for the relationship have NEVER matched the man I was dating. I am not perfect by a long shot, as you have read in the pages of this book, but just because I was raised in chaos does not mean I want to live my life in chaos. Dating has been a constant battle because I know what I desire in my heart, but I have a magnet on me that attracts narcissistic, selfish, and disrespectful men. I pride myself on giving my all in everything I do, which means when I love, I love hard.

But instead of men appreciating this rare quality, they take advantage of it. After the divorce, I started dating this older gentleman. When the relationship started, he did and said all the right things. I assumed that with age came a certain level of wisdom and maturity. Boy, was I wrong, again! He was truly kind and nurturing, much like my father, but that soon changed.

Brotherman started being verbally abusive, controlling, and offensive. It took me a while to figure out he was a narcissist. After dating him, I started studying the characteristics and traits of a narcissist. I did not want to experience that type of drama ever again in life. So, I had to learn the hard way that age has nothing to do with crazy. Older men have little boy syndrome too.

After escaping the narcissist, I was back at square one. I was left still searching outwardly for what I thought would ease the inward pain, fear, and loneliness. Pain from trusting that another broken person could help put my broken pieces back together. Fear of constantly doubting myself and rehearsing the failures from my past. And the loneliness I felt in between relationships because I still battled with abandonment issues.

Then 2017 rolled around, and I met this guy. He was rough and rugged around the edges, but he had a swag about him that was different from the rest of the guys I dated. I am not afraid to admit that I fell hard. Like they say, "opposites attract," and he was the total opposite from me. As always, the relationship started with the imposter.

The longer you be around a person, the more you get to know them. Well, getting to know him was not the only problem. He had a bitter ex-girlfriend who refused to let go. I mean, she was holding on as if her life depended on his presence. This woman did everything within her power to make my life a living hell. I did not know which was worse, her or my uncle, because they ran neck and neck with the manipulation and control issues.

She terrorized my family every day for two years straight. Not only did she hack my social media accounts, but she also spray-painted my car. My son received scholarships for basketball, and she tried to get them revoked by forging documents with my signature. I had to get a lifetime restraining order against this woman because she would not stop harassing us.

I dealt with this trauma for almost four years. She even tried to ruin my business and reputation by telling people I had a disease to stop them from coming to the shop. I could not believe that someone would go to these drastic measures behind a man. This woman wanted to destroy me, and she almost won–but GOD!

You must be very careful in life because the enemy is aware of your weakness, even when you are not. After all I went through with the ex-husband and the other failed relationships, I should have run at the first sight of drama, but I was mesmerized. He was like a drug, and I was addicted to the toxicity. The door to their relationship never closed because when I got tired, he ran back to her, and when he was tired of her, he ran back to me.

Just one big cycle of dysfunction, and be mindful I was still working, kids in school, battling Crohn's, and trying to be there for my mother all while being harassed and drug through the mud by another unstable brother. I hear you! Yes, I chose to stay in the relationship as long as I did and to be honest, I have no idea why.

Maybe I will blame it on Betty Wright, who said, "Having a piece of man is better than having no man at all." Nah! Well, it sounded good, but the truth is dysfunction attracts dysfunction. He had his undealt traumas, and I had mine. We did the best we could with the bit of sanity we had, but two is company, and three's a crowd. So, I started praying and asking God to help me escape this ungodly attachment.

In this relationship, the blind was leading the blind, and we both landed in the ditch. I had to cry out to God at this point because I was weak. The trauma bond with him and the ex drained the life out of me. I started having problems in the salon with people I thought I could trust. I mean one thing after another. One storm passed over, and but shortly after, another was coming in. I had no more fight left. I was left lifeless.

I threw up the white towel and surrendered. My mind, heart, body, soul, and spirit were worn out. I started spending more time alone and seeking God even more because I needed answers. I needed the roller coaster ride to end. I did not want to play on the merry-go-round anymore. It was fun in the beginning, but new things get old quickly. And this part of the story was becoming repetitive and boring. I was tired of hearing myself sing the same sad song, so I could only imagine what the listeners were thinking when I went crying on their shoulders.

It dawned on me that it was time to stop focusing on everything and everyone but me. I did not stay in the toxic relationship thinking about myself. I was thinking about him and his needs. I always gave more than I received.

What would he do without me? How would he make it? How would he survive? Well, I finally found peace in the fact that he was a grown man who was making it before me, and he would make it after me. See, ladies, and gents, this is where we mess up! We go over and beyond to take care of everyone before taking care of ourselves. Then we get mad when the person fails to reciprocate the care back to us.

As much as I hate to say this, we create this dynamic when we attempt to fill our inner emptiness by trying to fulfill the voids of others. No one, and I mean no one, can reach those places but GOD!

Chapter Nine
Changing The Narrative

Jesus said to her, "Did I not tell you that if you believed, you would see the glory of God?"
John 11:40

Stories change all the time. Have you ever heard a story from one person, but the storyline changed when you listened to the same story from a different person? I have experienced this a lot in life, but it taught me that people relay stories based on their understanding of what they heard because it is all about perception.

As I mentioned in previous chapters, life changed my perception in many ways. I spent my life in bondage to pain and rejection because my perception was based on experience and what I witnessed throughout my life. But there were other ways to perceive life of which I was unaware. Every time I told my story, it was through the lens of pain. I expressed my anger, rage, hurt, regret, and disappointment like a broken record to anyone willing to listen. It never dawned on me that I had the power to change the narrative. I never imagined talking about my life from a positive perspective when mostly everything was negative.

Let's take my uncle, for example. That was a horrible time in my life, but today I can honestly say it shifted something in my life. What the enemy meant for evil, God used it for His good. He got me out of that church before He tore it down, and my faith in Him was ruined based on the perception of my uncle as a man of God. I cannot say that for everybody because many worshiped the man versus worshipping God, which causes men to lose heart.

Abba Father wrote your script long before you were conceived, but the enemy has been rewriting scenes your whole life. Scenes where we simply step into the roles without question. We end up in bed with people we do not know. We find ourselves on track to be holy and righteous but end up playing the character of someone cold, hateful, and heartless. Can you imagine the situations I have been in when I acted a plum fool only to turn around and say, "that was not me" or "I don't act like that?"

You can become a character and fool people all day, including yourself, but the truth hurts. The fruits of your life will show up and show others that you are not authentic. Only how you live for God will make a difference. When I finally settled down long enough to eat and digest this kingdom principle, my life turned in a different direction.

The foundation of my life was broken before I even entered the world. Then as I grew older, I attempted to build upon a foundation that would never sustain the life I desired to live. So, I decided to change the narrative of my story to recreate a solid foundation for the future I envisioned. I despised the idea of becoming a family statistic. So, I had to fight hard to keep the bloodline demons at bay.

I stopped trying to see the glass full when it was bone dry. Even I was empty! Everything and everyone around me were empty, or should I say dead or asleep? My spiritual and natural eyes were closed to the demonic doors that were opened in my life through my bloodline and those that I opened on my own. I fought tooth and nail for almost thirty years of my life, trying to love and be loved. Needing the validation of a human being, and it never worked in my favor.

I just wanted to be seen and heard. I wanted to feel like I mattered to someone, anyone. My mother did the best she could, but I needed her validation as a child and to also be taught that true validation comes from God. I needed to know I was special and worthy of true love that was unattached to pain.

Hardcore life lessons stopped me from longing for this validation when I realized I was searching in the wrong places. I was trying to make a withdrawal from people who were mentally, spiritually, and emotionally bankrupt. It was like squeezing blood from a turnip, as they say. Nothing was happening, and nothing from nothing leaves nothing.

The story about Lazarus in the bible will have you scratching your head. There are so many twists and turns, but the end result is impressive. John 11 tells the story of Lazarus, the brother of Mary and Martha, who died and was raised from the dead by Jesus. Now I want you to pay close attention to the fact that this man was dead. As a matter of fact, he was dead for four days. Plus, he was a dear friend to Jesus.

When Jesus heard about His friend Lazarus, the bible says, "Jesus wept" and went to where he was buried. As he traveled to the gravesite, Martha met Jesus and said, "Had you been here, my brother would be alive!" Is it just me, or have you made this same statement? "God, if you had done this, my child would still be here, my marriage would still be intact, my money wouldn't be funny."

Jesus kept walking to the tomb, but then Mary approached Him and said the same thing Martha said. He continued to the grave and instructed the onlookers to roll the stone away. Martha stood there telling Jesus there would be an odor since he had been there four days. She was basically saying nothing could be done, his life was over. Jesus responded to her doubt by saying, *"Did I not tell you that if you believed, you would see the GLORY of God?"*

Lazarus stood there wrapped in grave clothes when Jesus said, "Lazarus come forth!" When He called him by name, Lazarus woke up, and Jesus said He was not dead, he was sleeping, and Lazarus lived. Jesus changed the narrative of Lazarus' story. All the naysayers and onlookers were focused on the natural aspect of death, but Jesus was focused on the power He possessed in the spirit to produce life and that more abundantly.

Jesus is the solution to every problem. After Jesus raised Lazarus, I can only imagine the look on Mary and Martha's faces. All they had to do was believe in order to see the salvation of the Lord. I experienced some dead stuff in my life that needed to stay dead, but then some things were sleeping and just needed to be called by name to wake up. I had to believe in the power of God to wake me up because I was fading fast.

All I had to do was surrender to the problem solver. I was so busy being a spectator in my own story that I was not playing the parts that were predestined for my life. I was trying to be the character in everyone else's story, and the plot thickened for the worse. When I look back, trouble met me when I was in the wrong place at the wrong time. Being out of alignment with God is dangerous.

I spent many years professing death over my life because I lacked spiritual confidence. I thought being a DIVA was enough to fill the empty places, but when I got home and removed the makeup and clothes, the real me, the broken me, would show up every time. There were times when I felt helpless and hopeless. Times when I felt defeated even though I was winning in certain areas. But God showed up and If He never did another thing for me, I can say He has done more than enough.

When I was lost in sin and trying to find my way, He never left me. Jesus set me free a long time ago, and when I was willing to hear His voice over man's voice, He called me by name, and I finally responded. I gave Him a sure yes from the depths of my soul, and that is when I woke up.

That is when I shook off those old dirty grave clothes (pain, shame, guilt, rejection, trauma, regret, and abandonment) and accepted the fact that God redeemed me. I became a new creature, saved by grace. Not only did He save me, but He has allowed His glory to manifest in every area of my life. I would not be who I am without the glory of God radiating in my life.

I could be very bitter and angry to this day, but I realized a long time ago that stress not only kills you, but it makes you look old. Having my first child at fourteen taught me how to persevere, endure, and always push hard. Even though I dropped out in middle school after getting pregnant, I decided to get my GED. It took some time, but I set my heart on creating a better life and example for my kids. How could I teach them about the importance of education when I dropped out?

I had to make this right, and I did. Many people are stuck because they are either afraid to try or feel as if it is too late. As long as God gives you breath in your body, it is never too late. Stop waiting on people to create opportunities you have the power to create for yourself through the mercy and favor of God.

I have been a stylist for almost thirteen years. I wanted to give up and throw in the towel several times, but I kept pushing. I had to work in other people's salons and pay them booth rent while dealing with unnecessary drama and foolishness. But during the completion of this book, God blessed me to open my own salon making six figures.

Again, if you forgot, I dropped out in the seventh grade and had a baby at fourteen, but today I am building an empire to leave a legacy behind. God blessed me with four beautiful children who have kept me rooted and grounded. They are my reason why! It is impossible to live life effectively without knowing why you are living.

God has not only shown up as my Father but as an amazing provider! When He speaks a prophetic word, you better take heed and patiently wait for the manifestation. My Father started prophetically speaking professional basketball over my son's life from the time he was fourteen. He is currently 6'9 and plays college basketball for Penny Hardaway at the University of Memphis. This has indeed been a blessing for our family.

Then there is my oldest son, who is currently serving six years on a twelve-year sentence for bank robbery. He is a good kid who got involved with the wrong crowd. My son graduated from school and moved to Atlanta with his best friend to pursue a career in music. He was so talented that he wrote and engineered his own music while working for some top people in the industry.

His best friend continued the path of music but recently passed away, and I cannot help but think that God had to allow my son to travel this path to save his life. We as humans tend to think we know what is best, but our mediocre thinking only leads to destruction. It is imperative to communicate with God because your life will never have a sense of direction without the word. You will drift and wander until you surrender!!

I never saw anything positive for my future. I mean NEVER! I am not telling you to surrender because it sounds good. I am telling you because that is what changed my life. I am not perfect by far. I still battle with all sorts of things, but I stay in my Father's face. I keep a humble heart, and I keep it REAL! God loves honesty. He said we must worship Him in SPIRIT and TRUTH. You can make your lips say a lot of things, but God is checking out your heart.

If I could leave you with some final words of wisdom. I would have to say, and I quote, "Experience is NOT always the best teacher!" Everything in life was not meant to learn the hard way. If this was true, then why do we need the bible. We bump our heads and make life complicated because we choose to follow a man and not God. You can follow the yellow brick road if you want to and end up like Dorothy, who, after all that traveling found out the wizard had NO POWER.

She still had to tap her shoes three times, speak her need out of her mouth, close her eyes, and believe. She had the power to make it home the whole time, but she kept falling for the illusions, and this is exactly how the enemy does us. We travel through life thinking we are powerless while waiting on permission from a man to do what God has already put in us. Some of you just need to close your eyes, put your vision before you, and believe that it will manifest in due time. There are no quick fixes in life. Some things require process and patience.

God is the ultimate storyteller who knows your beginning, middle, and end. All He wants from you and me is to TRUST THE PROCESS! Yes, life is all about the process. You will never have all the answers, but God never required you to.

Creating a new narrative started with a clear headspace. I had to turn the page to start a new chapter. I had erased and rewritten over the old pages for so long that there was nothing left. There is nothing like the smell of fresh paper and a new ink pen. Writing the new chapter meant I could no longer focus on the old. I had to break all covenants and soul ties to move forward.

I gave God His rightful place in my heart, and He became intimately acquainted with every detail of my life, and I am grateful. The Holy Spirit is a gentleman who will never invade your space. You must invite Him in, and when I presented the invitation, we are now in constant fellowship. My day begins and ends with talking to my Daddy!

When I learned to find my strength in God, I stopped talking to people and went straight to the Source. He said, "Draw near to Me, and I will draw near to you!" I find peace in His presence through worship and the word. The best thing you could ever do to obtain success in your life is to...COME TO HIM AS YOU ARE!

Stand in and tell your truth, and I guarantee you, He will shine His GLORY upon YOUR story!

Author Bio

Samantha Williams

Samantha is a force to be reckoned with as a woman who has defied the odds in many areas of her life. She was born and raised in Third Ward, Texas.

Samantha started her journey as an assistant to her cousin Misty, where she discovered her love for cosmetology. In 2006 she enrolled in Franklin Beauty School, graduating in 2008.

And she has been in the beauty industry for 14 years.

Continuing her education, Sam frequently traveled with world-renowned Hair/Makeup Artist Patric Bradley, Karlene Bethea, and many others to different hair shows perfecting her craft. She currently resides in Houston, Texas, with her kids and her mother.

Contact Information

Email: samanthastylez0@gmail.com

Website: www.samanthastylez.com

Facebook: @samanthahealthyhairstylistwilliams

Instagram: @samantha_stylez